Fortune Cookies

Volume 4

Dr. Kareem Pottinger

YSD Publishing House

Library of Congress Catalog in
Publication Data

YSD PUBLISHING HOUSE
14490 Coastal Bay Circle 13204
Naples, FL. 34119

Library of Congress Catalog Card
Number:
2013934185
International Standard Book
Number 978-1-937171-03-2

Dedicated to my firstborn

YOUNGSABATH POTTINGER

If I ever leave this planet, I have
always kept you in mind.

Not leavening my wisdom far behind

Grow Good

INTRODUCTION

The true intent of this book
was to write a set of guidelines
that could be
immediately implemented in
the progress and advancement
of my sons elite
life.
This vast deep knowledge was
to be used as a
tool
to keep him far beyond just,
"ahead of the learning curb" for
lack of better expression.
These
rules are the widely accepted
and used unspoken
secrets amongst the elite in
which we use to rear our

young.
Although these are our
secrets
and most of us will and should
be extremely displeased for
having them on display for the
"normal's" of the world to
receive, I decided to release
them nevertheless.
For,
upon reading the finished
piece I realized that these elite
secrets
could not only serve to benefit
my son and family to come
well, but that the entire
world
could serve to benefit from
these lists of guidelines.
The way that this book is
intended to be received is to

ponder upon each page for a complete 24 hours.

Each page is to be pondered upon for the whole day; it is to be used as topic of discussion for that day amongst peers, friends, and family members' etcetera.

It is especially designed to be pondered upon mostly by you. For a complete 24 hours deep thought on each subject should be pondered upon. The reason being is to see how these guidelines could be implemented into your current life, how should they have been implemented in your past life, and how can they benefit your future.

It
is only through the true
belief
and usage of these
guidelines
that your life's
works will be greatly
affected
in its progress.

Your
life
will
end-up
where
your
brain
takes
it

Personal experience is vital; you cannot just trust other people's judgment upon the things that are unknown to you, as factual

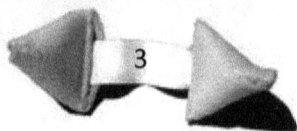

Manage your expectations

When you
are not
the
decision-maker,
you
have to
learn how to
take what
you can
get when you
can get it

*No
knowledge
that you
gain
will
outweigh
the
knowledge
that
you
receive through
experience*

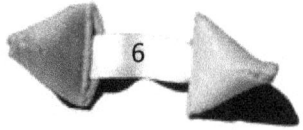

Whether
big, small,
more-than,
or
not-enough
at all,
you are going
to
have
to
start
somewhere

Whatever it is;
if you are
going
to do
it
right,
then
you will
need
to have
a
plan

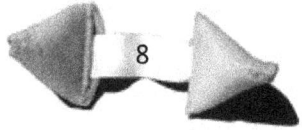

*Those
that follow
their
passions in life,
end-up
happier with
their
lives
do
to
less
regrets*

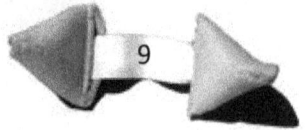

The greatest-sin that you can commit is a sin against yourself and to ignore the impulses of one's heart could be considered as sin

Envy means;
if they aren't
going to win,
then
nobody's
going to win
and that is an
extremely
dangerous
attitude to have
directed
towards you

*Simple
is
best;
get
in,
get
out,
and
go
home*

*There isn't a
such thing
as
perfectly safe,
which is
why
you shouldn't
have a
problem
with
taking
risk*

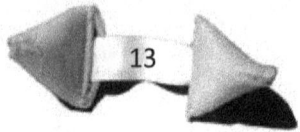

As long
as
you
have
life
in
you,
then there
is
hope
for you in your
cause

*Never
like
to
create
more
work
for
yourself
than is
necessary
to
create*

15

*It's your choice
to become
who you
would like
to become in
life
and
it is your
decision
whether you
become it
or not*

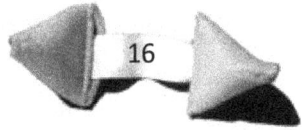

The only way to become truly free in life is by obtaining the type of success that will give you total independence

*Being aware of
the fact that;
some people
partner-up
for
money
and a position
in life, will
make it that
much harder for
someone to use
you*

You should
never want to
put
yourself
in a
position
where you can
get
caught
off-guard
and
unprotected

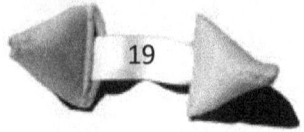

*The best
kept
secrets
will
always
be
the
ones
that
you
never
tell*

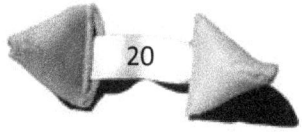

Your
path
of
tomorrow
is
being
created
by
you
today

Be aware that your views do change on any particular subject depending on the amount of facts that you know about that subject

22

*Anything
that you
want deeply
enough, is
worth
the
chance
that
you
have
too
take*

*The risk takers
are the people
that
"score-big",
you
just
have to be
smart
about
the
risk that
you take*

*Take your
small
gift
that
you
have
and
polish
it
until
it
shines*

*Be aware that
your life
will
fly by you,
when you
don't have your
steps
in order
and
you are not
doing anything
of value*

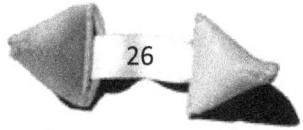

You need too get rid-off all the broken links in your life, because every link in your chain must work in order for your whole system to work to its fullest potential

*In order to get
the big
fish,
you
need
to
catch
some
of
the
smaller
ones*

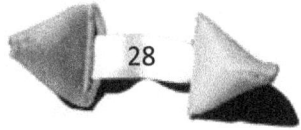

*When deciding
whether to
take action
or
not,
you should
always
look at
the
risk
verses
the return*

As you allow
time
to pass by
without
accomplishing
anything
towards your
dream,
your dream
starts
to
die

In regards to accomplishing your goals; you should focus more on productivity rather than activity

Everything
happens
in
the
order
in
which
you
allow
it
to
transpire

32

*It is important
to know
that
human-beings
are
constantly
demonstrating
on the outside,
what is
going
on
in the inside*

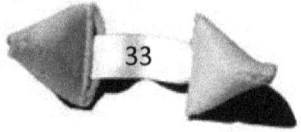

*Understand
that
behind every
effect,
there is
an
exact equal
cause
that
projects
that
effect*

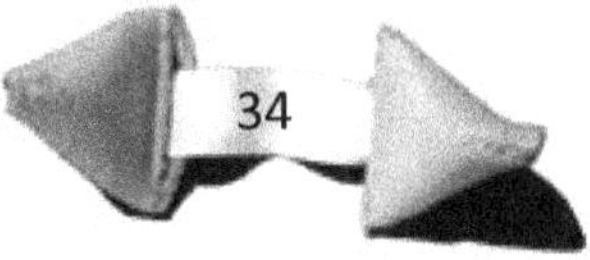

*No favor
that you
will
ever
perform
for
another,
will
go
unpunished*

*In a team
or
partnership;
when
one is
weak
it
will
make
the
rest
weak*

*Dreams can
only get
you so
far,
then
after
that
you are
going
to
need
cash*

*The more
that
you know
about what is
ahead,
the better
that you
can
plan
for what
is
ahead*

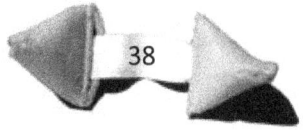

You
should
never
say
anything
that
you
might
regret
later

You
have
to
surrender
yourself
to
a
plan,
in
order
to
succeed

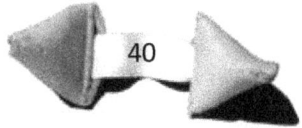

*It
will
always
take
some
money
in order
to
make
more
money*

*Certain things
are so
unpredictable
that
you
can
blink
your
eye
and
everything
changes*

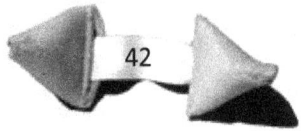

*For your
life,
you should
want
to
have
the absolute
best
of
everything
that you can
have*

When you really start to realize who you are and who you can become, that is the exact moment you begin to climb that mountain towards the top

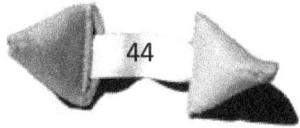

*Depending
upon
the
phrasing
of
your
questions,
you can
find out
all
the
answers*

*Never
take
a
job
that
you
cannot
complete*

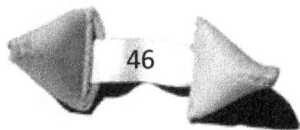

*If you
swallow
everything
in
sight,
it will
only be a
matter of
time
before
you
throw-up*

*You
have to have
an aim
in
whatever it is
that you are
doing,
when you
want whatever
that your doing
to turn out
great*

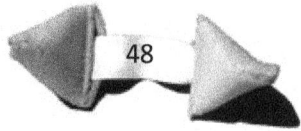

*In life; in order
to succeed
in a
great way,
you
have to be
unafraid
to make
a
different-kind
of
mistake*

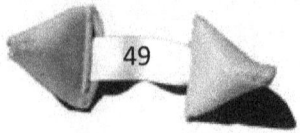

*Depending
upon
how much
you
believe in
yourself; that is
what
will determine
whether
you succeed
or
not*

50

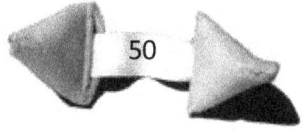

*Life
is
the
best
gift
ever
given
to
you,
so
enjoy
it*

*A
sinking-ship
is
not
something
that
you
should
want
to
jump
aboard*

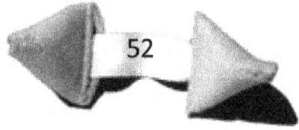

*Where you
end-up
in life
is not
random;
you direct your
life which way
you want it
to go,
much like you
would direct a
steering wheel*

53

*Be
cautious
of
putting
your
faith
into
trinkets
of
deceit*

The luckiest
person
on the face
of the
earth,
is
the
one
that
finds
true
love

*Make
the
maximum
profit
out
of
others
combined
stupidity*

*Being
very-smart
and
extremely
careful
is what
you need
to be
when
taking
a
huge risk*

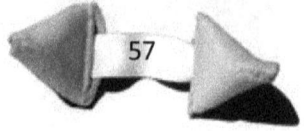

It is always important to take the time-out for yourself, to do something that you have never done before

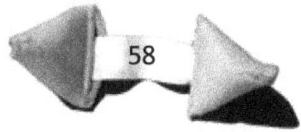

When you have
a
problem,
the
first-thing
you need to do
is to
stop
making
that
problem
worse

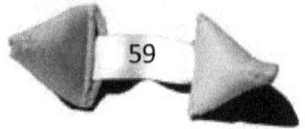

*The
only
people
that
can
make
us
free,
are
ourselves*

*Take care
of
your
mistakes
before
they
take care
of
you*

*Always
keep in mind
that all
walks
of
life
will
continue
to do
what they
want
to do*

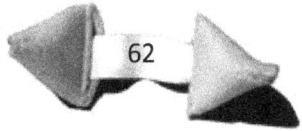

*There is no
exception,
everyone
will
pay the
price
for the things
that they
want
or
they will not
get them*

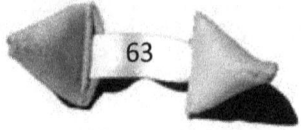

*Sometimes
you just
have to
play-out
a
bad
hand,
in order
to learn
something
of
deeper value*

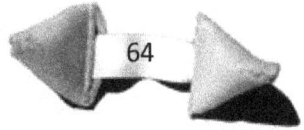

You shouldn't practice to do any favors and you should not ask for any either

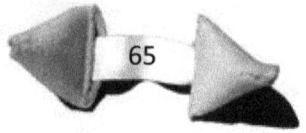

You should always watch what other-people do, much more than you listen to what they say

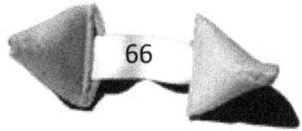

*Always
watch
your
percentages*

*Learn
to
appreciate
what
you
have,
while
you
still
have
it*

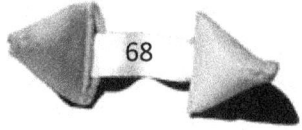

*Everyone in
life
has their
own
bad-habits,
you just
have to
be
smart
enough
to get
rid-of them*

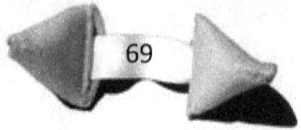

*You are
to
always
trust
your
instincts,
that
is
why
you
have them*

In
the
heat
of
the
moment,
it is
always
easy
to
lose
perspective

It is more common in life for people to turn-out worse than you think they truly-are, rather than those people to turn-out better than you think they truly-are

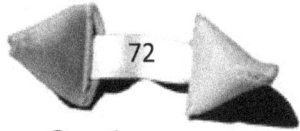

Get rid-of the garbage that is in your life immediately after you realize that it is garbage, because garbage tends to make the things that it is closet to stink when you allow it to linger

*No matter
how low
you
sink, it is
important to
remember that
there still
remains
a
right
from
wrong*

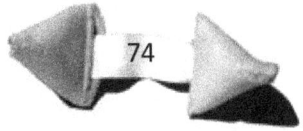

*Learn to
change
the
channel
of your
life,
when
your
television-show
begins
to
suck*

*The coward
never even
starts-out
what they
set to
accomplish
and
that is a
characteristic
that you should
never want to
absorb*

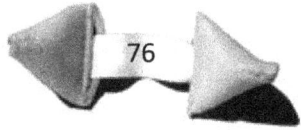

*We are all
pretty-small
in the bigger-
scheme of things
and the sooner
that you are able
to understand
this, the more
you will be able
to notice the
universal-signs
that most are
unable to see*

*The
weak-ones
will
always
die-off
on
the
road
to
success*

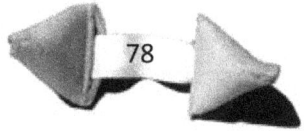

Destiny and
where
you
end-up
in
life,
is only
a matter
of the
choices
that
you make

*You have to be
strong
in
determination
and
persistence
when you want
to
arrive
and
achieve
your goals*

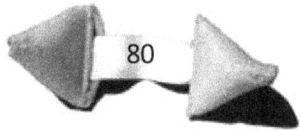

You have to learn how to reach for the things that you want and once this technique is mastered, you will quickly see that there is nothing that you cannot obtain

81

*Do not
let
anyone
fool you;
no one
does
anything
for nothing,
there is
always
a
trade-off*

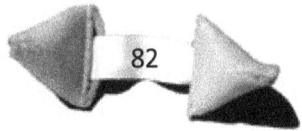

*Don't ever
let
someone
else
profit
from
their
scheming
on
you*

*A
true
collector
will
always
go
anywhere,
to
get
what
they
want*

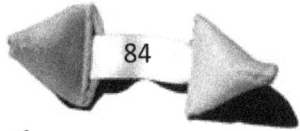

You should never want to possess a narrow mind when it comes down to making decisions and choosing options; but in its stead you should always keep your minds' eye open to the many different possibilities that are always out there

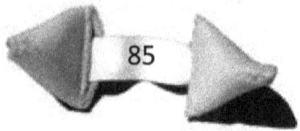

An
old
acquaintance
is
not
the
same
as
an
old
friend

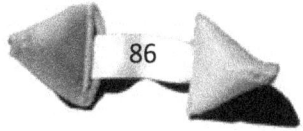

*Never
get
cute
with
someone
you
owe
money
too*

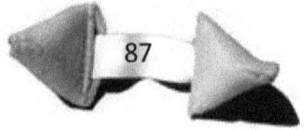

You should always keep belief and have hope in your cause, because sometimes that is the only determinate that will allow you to meet your vision

*Understand
that
when everyone
is
saying
the
same-thing,
there has
to be some
sense
of
truth to it*

As hard as you want it to work for you, that's how hard you have to work for it

It will
always
be
better
for
you
to
be
safe
rather
than
being sorry

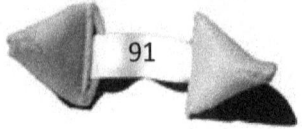

*Success
is
getting
up
more
times
than
you
fall*

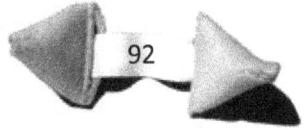

When failing in a particular agenda, sometimes it's all about just using your natural-attributes in a different way in order to succeed

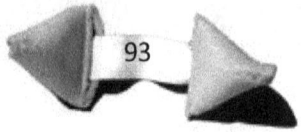

A
great-plan
is
always
an
adaptable-one,
any plan
that you
create
should
be
changeable

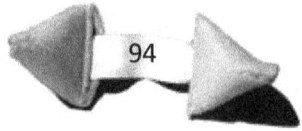

*It is
extremely
important
for
the health of
your
character
to allow
yourself
to be
who
you are*

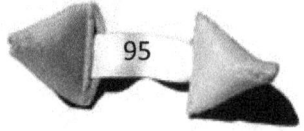

*In
dealing with
a spouse;
in order to
keep the
flame
going, you have
to
keep
them
off
balance*

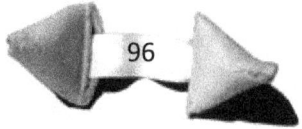

*You
have to
want
to
help
yourself,
in order
to
get
major
things
accomplished*

*Whenever
your
involved
with
quick-witted
people,
you must
always keep in
mind
that they can
get carried
away*

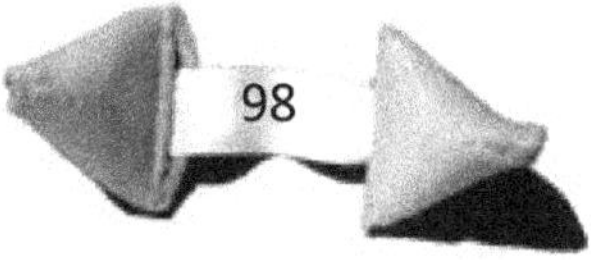

*You should
always
behave
as
your
heart
tells
you
is
best
to
behave*

*You have
to be
careful
with the
choice
of
people
that you
choose
to have
accompany
you in life*

Allow
yourself
to
be
yourself
and
you
will
always
be
free

In regards to those that follow and do not lead; you should keep in mind that the shadow of a person can never get-up and walk-off on its own

People in life will gather and scatter following their own personal interest, so don't get dismayed when someone doesn't stick around forever

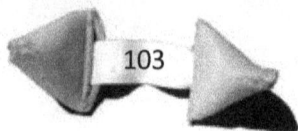

*You may
have to
take
a
step down,
in order
to
move
a
couple
steps
forward*

*To open your
eyes
and
look
for
yourself,
will
always
be
what is
best
for you*

*You
have to
be
able
to
learn
how
to
add
value
to
yourself*

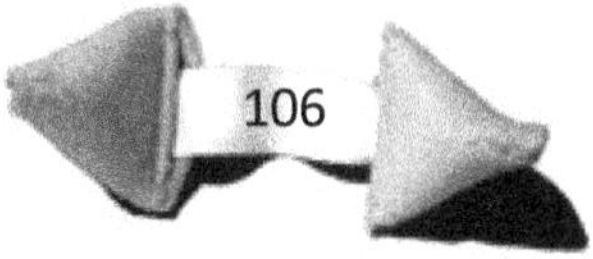

*The
best
accessory
you
can
ever
wear,
is
your
confidence*

When you are in the vicinity of garbage; regardless of how clean you are you will start to stink like that garbage and because of this, you should stay away from garbage

When you're
flying
by the seat of
your
pants,
nothing
sounds
more
official
than
a
plan B

*Sometimes
you have
to narrow
your
focus
in
order
to
accomplish
your
short-term
goals*

When someone thinks they have you all figured-out, that's when they become most vulnerable to your whims

*There
will always be
a
reward
waiting
for those of
you that
take
full-advantage
of
your
foresight*

*Maintaining
long-term
diligence
and
pressure
is the
hard-part
of
obtaining any
goal
but it is an
absolute-must*

*Anything
that
you
commit
to
doing,
should
never
be
done
half-way*

*It is
important
for you
to
understand
that
easier
does
not
always
mean
better*

*The faster you
learn that
money
has a way of
corrupting
certain-peoples
principles,
the more
astute you will
become to the
signs of their
corruption*

*Some people
will not be able
to
make
clear-decisions
when
money
is
involved,
the money will
cloud their
judgment*

When you always help yourself when you can, where you can; you and everyone around you, will find that you are always evolving and improving

*The
worst-crime
that
you
can do
to
yourself,
is
to
waste
your
life*

*In life you
should
always
make
the
best
of
what
anyone
has too
offer
you*

*The sooner
you learn
that
things
always
seem
to
work
themselves out,
the calmer
your life will
become*

*It is extremely
important
to
know
if
the
equipment that
you are
going to use,
is
capable
or not*

*It is extremely
important
in life
to know
what you
do not want
in your life
and
how to keep
those things
out of your
life*

You will always
have to
work
towards
freedom,
it
will
never be
free
without any
effort from your
behalf

When you are trying to be an elusive target, you should never fly-straight but instead switch-lanes from time to time

*Greed
gets
the
best
of
everyone
who
participates
in
it*

*As
your
investments
grow
and
change
so
should
your
strategies*

*You will never
be able to
stop
the feelings
that are inside
of you
and once you
remain true to
those feelings,
you will remain
true to
yourself*

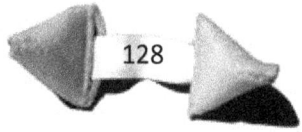

Sometimes
the
best-way
for
someone
to
learn
is
the
hard-way

A person

is

and

can

only

become

as

big

as

they

are

thinking

*To
obtain
being
sure,
is
one
of the
finest
goals
that you
can
possess*

To know where the power is located is equal to having access to that power, because you will only need to get there in order to access it

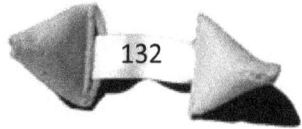

*It will always
be
better
for you
to
try and fail
rather
than
for you
to not
have tried
at all*

The bad-parts
of your life are
personally for
you to help
grow,
you should
keep them
private and
only express
the good that
you have learnt
through the bad

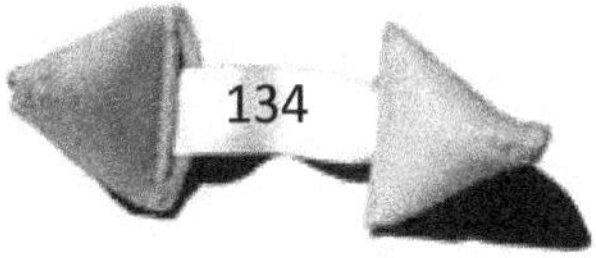

*You
will
pay
for
your
lack
of
knowledge,
everyone
in
life
does*

Quitting
along
the way
to
your
destination
will
never
get you
to
your
destination

*Something's
may have to
fall-apart
in your
life
so that other
more
important
things
can fall
into
place*

*Many
things that you
do not like
about your life
will never
change
until
you
make
the effort
to
change it*

*Sometimes
the
smartest
remark
that you
can ever
make
is
no
remark
at
all*

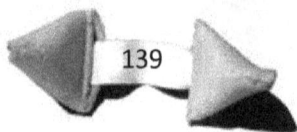

*In
life,
do not
go
for
the
plum
that
has
already
been
bitten*

*The
better you
look;
the bigger
the
money
that you
can get
closer too,
so
fix yourself
up*

*You can never
judge
a persons
power
by their
appearance
alone, many
people use
optical-illusions
to mask the
sense of their
power*

142

*Victory
does
not
always belong
to the
powerful
but
will always
belong
to those that
use
their smarts*

*We as people
all
stumble
from
time to time,
the point of the
stumbling is to
learn how to
use those
stumbling-
blocks as
stepping-stones*

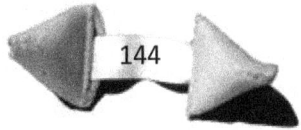

*Anything
to
win,
is
the
attitude
of
the
person
that
wins*

Anyone
can
start
but
only
the
finishers
are
successful

*Those
that
listen
will learn
how
to
become
better
than
what
they
are*

*If you don't let
fear
control you;
then your
life
becomes
simple;
you make
decisions
and
don't
look-back*

In life;
you have to get
committed
to
raising
your
lifestyle
in order
to
raise
your
lifestyle

When your living in the moment; there is no past, no future, and no problems

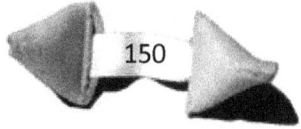

*50
percent
of
something
will always
be
better
than
100
percent
of
nothing*

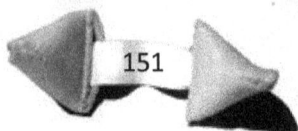

*You
are
responsible
for
your
own
mess*

Who
you
choose
to
be
around,
lets
you
know
who
you
are

*Even though
you may not
see it,
every
challenge
that
you
face
creates
an
opportunity
to be had*

*The
sign
of
good
decision-
making
is
success
and
progress*

Always control your emotions because it is very simple to be exploited by them

*Your
metal
will
get
tested
during
times
of
crisis,
be
prepared*

*Efficiency
is
key;
no matter
what you are
doing,
it will
always
come-down
to
time
management*

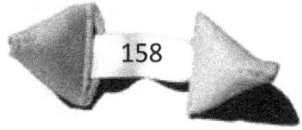

In life you should not want to have any internal in-harmony because any internal in-harmony that you posses will attract external in-harmony into your life

The end

Additional books written by

Dr. Kareem Pottinger available online at

www.FORTUNECOOKIES.me

and your local book stores nationwide

<u>FORTUNE COOKIES VOLUMES 1-11</u>

also

available

on

your

<u>Kindle</u>

<u>Nook</u>

<u>Apple</u>

<u>devices</u>

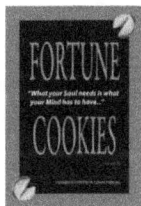

www.ingramcontent.com/pod-product-compliance
Lightning Source LLC
Chambersburg PA
CBHW030104070426
42448CB00037B/958